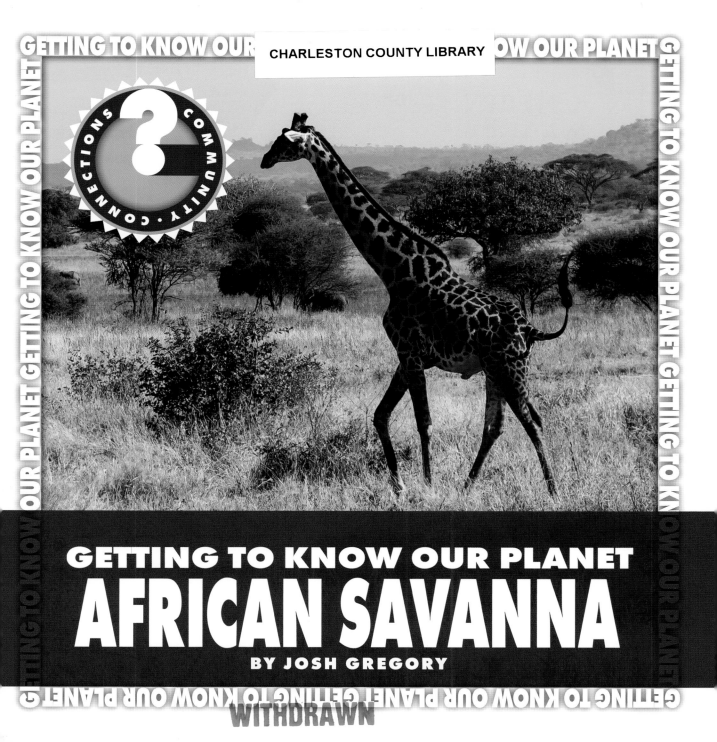

GETTING TO KNOW OUR PLANET
AFRICAN SAVANNA

BY JOSH GREGORY

Published in the United States of America by Cherry Lake Publishing
Ann Arbor, Michigan
www.cherrylakepublishing.com

Content Adviser: Linda M. Hooper-Bùi, PhD, Associate Professor, Department of
Environmental Science, Louisiana State University Agricultural Center, Baton Rouge, Louisiana
Reading Adviser: Marla Conn, Read With Me Now

Photo Credits: Cover and page 1, © Lizzy Phelan/Shutterstock.com; page 5, © Black Sheep
Media/Shutterstock.com; pages 7 and 11, © Vadim Petrakov/Shutterstock.com;
page 9, © GFC Collection/Alamy Stock Photo; page 13, © Pal Teravagimov/Shutterstock.com;
page 15, © Mikhail Turkeev/Shutterstock.com; page 17, © Oleg Znamenskiy/Shutterstock.com;
page 19, © Magdalena Paluchowska/Shutterstock.com; page 21, © John Wollwerth/
Shutterstock.com.

LIBRARY OF CONGRESS CATALOGING-IN-PUBLICATION DATA
Names: Gregory, Josh author.
    Title: African Savanna / by Josh Gregory.
Description: Ann Arbor, Michigan : Cherry Lake Publishing, [2015] |
    Series: What's it like to live here? | Series: Community connections |
    Includes bibliographical references and index.
Identifiers: LCCN 2015023297| ISBN 9781634705127 (lib. bdg.) |
    ISBN 9781634706322 (pbk.) | ISBN 9781634705721 (pdf) |
    ISBN 9781634706926 (e-book)
Subjects: LCSH: Savanna ecology—Africa—Juvenile literature. | Savanna animals—Africa—
    Juvenile literature. | Grasslands—Africa—Juvenile literature.
Classification: LCC QH194 .G73 2015 | DDC 577.4/8—dc23 LC record available
at http://lccn.loc.gov/2015023297

Cherry Lake Publishing would like to acknowledge the
work of The Partnership for 21st Century Skills. Please
visit www.p21.org for more information.

Printed in the United States of America
Corporate Graphics
January 2016

AFRICAN SAVANNA

CONTENTS

A WIDE-OPEN SPACE

Take a look around the **savanna** in Africa's Serengeti National Park. The landscape stretches as far as your eyes can see. You spot a few trees and bushes here and there. But most of the area is covered in tall grass. The land is mostly flat, but you can see small hills in the distance. What an incredible view!

A savanna is a type of grassland.

What do you already know about the African savanna? What do you want to learn more about? Write down your questions. See if you find the answers in this book.

The weather in a savanna is always warm. During the summer, it rains a lot. The rest of the time, it might not rain at all. In fact, a savanna might go 2 to 11 months without rain.

There are savannas in many parts of the world. The largest savannas are in Africa.

Sometimes rain can be seen coming from great distances in the savanna.

MAKE A GUESS!

Wildfires are common in many savannas. Why do you think this is? Think about the weather and types of plants found in a savanna.

GRASS, GRASS EVERYWHERE

The most common plants in the savanna are grasses. Some types of grasses are short. They may be just a few inches high. Most grasses in Africa's savanna are very tall. Elephant grass can grow to be 10 feet (3 meters) high! Its roots are long, which allows it to reach water deep underground. It can get water even when the weather is very dry.

Elephant grass is named after the elephant. Like the grass, this animal is known for its size.

Different kinds of plants grow in different environments. Look at the plants growing near your home. Are they different from plants in a savanna? Are they similar? Is there a lot of grass near you? What does it look like?

Most savannas also have many different trees and bushes. Savannas with more rain usually have more trees than drier savannas. Bushes are more common in African and other dry savannas. These savannas do have some trees, however. The acacia tree is one of Africa's most common types. Acacias have very small leaves and long, sharp spines. Their branches spread far out from the trunk.

The acacia tree is covered in spines. This helps protect the tree from most animals.

MAKE A GUESS!

Trees are less common than grass in savannas. This is because of the **biome**'s rainy and dry seasons. What might happen if a savanna had no dry season? Would there be more trees? Fewer trees?

11

AFRICAN ANIMALS

Africa's savannas are home to many kinds of animals. A giraffe's long neck helps it reach leaves in treetops. **Herds** of striped zebras and speedy gazelles roam open spaces. Enormous elephants suck water into their **trunks**. Then they spray it on themselves. This keeps the elephants cool.

A herd of zebras and wildebeest walk by a lake full of flamingos.

Some of the world's largest land animals live in the savanna. Why do you think this is? What does the savanna offer that large animals might need to survive?

13

Some savanna animals are deadly hunters. Cheetahs are among the fastest animals on Earth. They use their speed to chase down **prey**. Powerful lions hunt together in groups. This helps them take down huge animals such as wildebeest. **Agile** leopards climb trees. From there, they can pounce on prey.

A leopard watches for prey from its perch in a tree.

THINK!

Many savanna animals are **endangered**. Can you think of any possible causes for this? What are some human activities that might hurt these animals? How could we help protect the animals?

Not all animals in Africa's savannas are so large. Thousands of insect **species** also live there. There are huge beetles and colorful butterflies. Termites on the savanna build enormous dirt mounds to live in. A single termite is smaller than your fingernail. But a mound can be up to 17 feet (5 m) tall! Millions of termites live inside.

Termites work together to build a mound.

LOOK!

Go looking for insects in different kinds of outdoor areas. How many insects can you find? Are the insects in one area different from those in another? Do any of them look like insects in the African savanna?

HUMANS ON THE SAVANNA

People live on the African savanna, too. Most of them have lived the same way for hundreds of years. There are no big towns or cities. Instead, many people live in small villages. Others are **nomads**. They do not have permanent homes.

The Maasai are nomads. They move from place to place with their cattle.

THINK!

Think about what it might be like to live as a nomad. Where would you sleep? Where would your food and water come from? What would it be like to travel so much?

19

Some people who live on the savanna have farms. They also raise livestock, such as sheep or goats. Other people hunt animals and gather wild plants to eat.

The African savanna is an incredible place. It is full of interesting people and amazing animals. Would you like to live there?

Some people in the savanna raise cattle. They rely on these animals for meat and milk.

Now you have
an idea of what a
savanna looks like.
Try drawing a picture
of one. Be sure to
include a variety of
plants, animals,
and people!

GLOSSARY

agile (AJ-il) able to move fast and easily

biome (BYE-ohm) a type of area on Earth that is organized by which plants and animals live there

endangered (en-DAYN-jurd) at risk of dying out completely

herds (HURDZ) large groups of animals that stay together

nomads (NOH-madz) members of a community that travels from place to place instead of living in one place

prey (PRAY) an animal hunted by another animal for food

savanna (suh-VAN-uh) a flat, grassy plain with few trees

species (SPEE-sheez) one of the groups into which living things are divided; members of the same species can mate and have offspring

trunks (TRUNKS) elephants' long noses

FIND OUT MORE

BOOKS

Kalman, Bobbie. *Baby Animals in Savanna Habitats*. New York: Crabtree, 2012.

Labella, Susan. *A Home on the Savanna*. New York: Children's Press, 2007.

WEB SITES

PBS—Savanna: The People

www.pbs.org/wnet/africa/explore/savanna/savanna_people_lo.html

Learn more about the different groups of people who call Africa's savannas home.

Pittsburgh Zoo—African Savanna

www.pittsburghzoo.org/animallist.aspx?c=2

Learn more about the animals of the African savanna.

INDEX

ABOUT THE AUTHOR

Josh Gregory is the author of more than 90 books for kids. He has written about everything from animals to technology to history. A graduate of the University of Missouri–Columbia, he currently lives in Portland, Oregon.

24